In Flame

Charlotte Jones trained as an actress. Her first play,
Airswimming, was premièred at the Battersea Arts
Centre, London. *In Flame* was premièred in January
1999 at the Bush Theatre, London, and revived at the
New Ambassadors, London, in September 2000. *Martha,
Josie and the Chinese Elvis* premièred at the Bolton
Octagon in April 1999 and transferred to the Liverpool
Everyman in May of that year. Charlotte Jones won the
Critics' Circle Award for Most Promising Playwright in
2000 for *In Flame* and *Martha, Josie and the Chinese
Elvis*.

CHARLOTTE JONES

In Flame

faber and faber

First published in 2000
by Faber and Faber Limited
3 Queen Square, London WC1N 3AU

Typeset by Country Setting, Kingsdown, Kent CT14 8ES
Printed in England by Intype London Ltd

A CIP record for this book
is available from the British Library

ISBN 0–571–20777–4

2 4 6 8 10 9 7 5 3 1

*For Elizabeth 'Molly' O'Keefe
and Ida Noreen Jones,
my grandmothers,
and Sophie Winter, my friend*

In Flame was first presented at the Bush Theatre, London, by St Elmo Productions, produced by Matthew Byam Shaw and Grant Parsons, on 13 January 1999. The cast was as follows:

Clara / Clootie Rosie Cavaliero
Frank / Mat Ivan Kaye
Annie / Gramma Marcia Warren
James / Arthur Tom Smith
Alex Valerie Gogan
Livvy Emma Dewhurst

Director Anna Mackmin
Designer Tom Pye
Lighting Sue Baynton, Flick Ansell
Choreographer Scarlett Mackmin
Composer Andy Cowton

The play was revived at the New Ambassadors Theatre, London, produced by Matthew Byam Shaw, Act, Lee Dean and ATG, on 4 September 2000. The cast was as follows:

Clara / Clootie Rosie Cavaliero
Frank / Mat Ivan Kaye
Annie / Gramma Marcia Warren
James / Arthur Jason Hughes
Alex Kerry Fox
Livvy Emma Dewhurst

Director Anna Mackmin
Designer Tom Pye
Lighting Jenny Kagan
Choreographer Scarlett Mackmin
Composer Andy Cowton

Characters

Clara / Clootie

Frank / Mat

Alex

Mother / Gramma

James / Arthur

Livvy

Act One

SCENE ONE

Thackley, 1908.
   Clara kneels listening to a wall. She can't quite believe what she's heard. Listens again. Then moves along to hear something else.
   Frank enters. He is a burly, good-looking man in his early thirties. He watches her. Suddenly she notices him.

Clara Oh!

Frank Don't mind me.

Clara I'm listening to the wall.

Frank So I see.

Clara (*suddenly suspicious*) You don't live in Thackley.

Frank No. I'm just passing through.

Clara Oh right.

   Pause.

Do you want to have a listen?

Frank Why not.

Clara This is a particularly good wall. Although they've most of them got sommat to say.

   He comes over.

Frank Here?

Clara Lower down. Can you hear?

Frank What?

Clara Sounds.

Frank Not a sausage.

Clara Wait a bit.

Frank What am I supposed to be listening out for, exactly?

Clara Shufty over. (*She listens next to him.*) There's all sorts here. Ladies singing and dancing. Music playing. You know. Lutes. A bit of poetry. (*She moves to a different place.*) Over 'ere there's a baby crying. (*She moves again.*) And over 'ere there's a man shouting his head off. An army in the distance. Drummin'. Marching. Battle. Bloodshed.

Frank What does bloodshed sound like?

Clara You know, moaning and wailing. Dying really slow.

Frank That's a lot of sounds for one little wall.

Clara Of course. It's all the secrets of this place, you see, when the people die, the secrets pass into the stone.

Frank Like osmosis.

Clara I don't think so.

Frank Let's have another listen.

Clara Did you hear that?

Frank What?

Clara A low rumbling.

Frank I think that was my stomach.

Clara (*sharply*) It's gone now anyway. You've got to be on your toes.

Frank Do you listen to walls a lot?

Clara I do.

Frank Must be exhausting.

Clara It is actually, 'specially 'cos you hear more sad things than happy things.

Frank Why?

Clara Because the sound of them lasts for longer.

Frank I wonder why I couldn't hear anything.

Clara You mustn't have the knack. Or else you didn't want to hear.

Frank I don't have your talent for wall listening.

Clara No. Only trouble with me is I hear all these things but then I just forget them.

Frank In one ear and out the other?

Clara That's right. I'm very good at hearing. But I'm even better at forgetting. That's all you're good for, Gramma says.

Frank Who's Gramma?

Clara She's my all and I'm her all except for Livvy. Our parents are dead.

Frank Oh. I forget everything too. All the time.

Clara It's good to forget things sometimes. Like Dilly Barley's dog. You can kick it and bite it and throw stones at it and the next time you see it, it wags and wags. It's a stupid dog.

Frank Yes.

Clara Gramma says that when you're born, the first instant of being a little baby you have a perfect memory. You remember everything about God and clouds and all the people who ever lived and all the happiness and sadness and recipes for cake and things and then after that it's just one long forgetting and forgetting and forgetting. Every day. Until you've forgotten everything and then you're ready to die so you can be born again and remember everything that you've ever forgotten.

Frank Is she very wise, your Gramma?

Clara Very. She's got a big oracle.

Frank Has she?

Clara Yes. It's like a telescope. Do you want to meet her?

Frank Ah. I don't know.

Clara You might have already met her.

Frank I don't think so.

Clara Sometimes you know people a long time before you meet them. And then you meet them and it's a surprise because you already know them really well.

Frank Is that so?

Clara (*she has taken a real shine to Frank*) Yes. Like you. I think maybe I've known you for ages. But we've only just met.

Frank That's nice.

Clara Yes. I'm Clara.

Frank Pleased to meet you again.

Clara What are you going to do for me now?

Frank I have to do something?

Clara Yes. Something special, since you're just passing through.

Frank I don't think I do anything special. No. Nothing that special.

Clara Oh.

Frank Sorry.

Clara I felt sure you could.

Frank No. For you I would. I certainly would. But I've got nothing up my sleeve today . . . I'll be off then.

Clara Maybe you've just forgotten it.

Frank What?

Clara The special thing you do. Maybe it's slipped your mind.

Frank I'm nothing special, Clara.

Clara Oh yes you are.

Frank Really I'm not.

Clara If you remember it, come back.

Frank What?

Clara Your special thing. I'll wait.

Frank Ay. I'll do that. (*He goes to exit.*) Clara's a very pretty name. It suits you.

Clara beams. Lights fade on her.

SCENE TWO

Alex's mother Anne shuffles on. She is in her early sixties. She has had a mild stroke which slightly restricts her movements. She also has Alzheimer's Disease. She is in a nursing home.

Mother
I could have danced all night
And still have begged for more
I could have spread my wings
And done a thousand things
I've never done before –

James, her care assistant who is in his early thirties enters during this.

James That's right, Annie. You raise the rafters.

Mother I pissed myself.

James Oh. Don't worry, petal, we'll soon have you sorted out. Just sit yourself down, lovey.

He starts to clean her up. She continues to sing, perhaps with more gusto.

Mother
I never knew what made it so exciting
Why all at once my heart took flight
I only know when he began to dance with me
I could have danced, danced, danced all night –

James (*during this*) Woops-a-daisy. There we go, pet. Now just wipe between your legs, Annie. Try and keep still. There's a good girl. Shall I put some talc there to dry you off? Don't want you getting sore. There, that's better.

Mother I was a dancer.

James Were you now?

Mother Tap dancer. Lovely pair of pins. Right up to my neck.

James We'd better get you some dry knickers, Annie.

Mother She did all the same steps as him.

James What?

Mother (*impatiently*) Ginger Rogers.

James Ah yes, Ginger Rogers and Fred Astaire. The same steps as Fred Astaire. Yes.

Mother But she did them backwards. On high heels. The men didn't do the hard stuff. It was all, one, two, swivel your head and present. No tricksy stuff. I liked dancing on my own the best.

James I bet you did. Right little rocker.

Mother You always had to smile. I didn't like that so much. But I miss the tap, tap, tap. My feet couldn't keep still. Even in bed they had a life of their own.

James That's great, Annie. We'll have to get you up and tapping. Entertain the troops.

Mother No, no, no. Not after she was born.

James Ah well, I've hung my dancing shoes up as well.

Mother I saw her. Ginger. She became a right bloater in the end, you know. Not even the dancing can save you.

James No, you're right there, Annie.

Mother Are you sure this is where I live now?

James Oh yes. You live here all right.

Mother What a doghole.

James No sitting on the fence for you, Annie, is there? We'd better get you spick and span for when Alex comes.

Mother Alex?

James Your daughter, Annie.

Mother Now you keep away from me. I'm not in the habit of giving strange men my knickers.

James That's a very wise policy, Annie. I'll leave some fresh out.

Mother (*sadly*) These shoes won't tap. No matter how hard you try.

James They're Hush Puppies, Annie.

Mother What?

James Hush Puppies.

Mother I don't know any.

James No, your shoes.

Mother I'm allergic to cats.

James Never mind. You keep singing, eh?

Mother Hum.

> *James exits.*
> *She suddenly lights up with a memory.*

I was magnificent. I was bloody magnificent.

SCENE THREE

Alex's flat. Alex is looking through some old photographs.
   Clootie enters in a flurry. She is slightly younger than Alex, plump and attractive.

Clootie Sometimes I want to push people out of the way. I'm not talking about nudging. I'm talking about shunting them. Right off the pavement.

Alex Hello Clootie.

Clootie And sometimes I want to push strangers under trains. That's bad, isn't it?

Alex Yes.

Clootie I mean I don't think I ever would.

Alex No.

Clootie Do you ever feel like that?

Alex No I don't.

Clootie I think I might be an evil person.

Alex I brace myself. On station platforms. Just in case.

Clootie Perhaps I've got a syndrome.

Alex No you haven't.

Clootie Like a screaming in church and pulling emergency cords in a non-emergency-situation-type syndrome.

Alex You've had a bad shift. You didn't get good tips.

Clootie I think I've developed road rage.

Alex You can't drive.

Clootie Pavement rage, then. Sometimes the way people walk really fucks me off.

Alex You're over-tired.

Clootie I work in a pie and cider restaurant. How on earth did that come to pass?

Alex You should look for something else.

Clootie All the people who eat there are mad. Serial killers. With rotting genitalia.

Alex You could do lots of things.

Clootie They only employ me because I make people feel better about ordering pudding.

Alex That's not true.

Clootie I mean I went to university. The world was once allegedly my oyster.

Alex You just haven't found your niche.

Clootie I can't do any more courses, Alex. Or anything that involves a gym.

Alex Don't worry. It'll come to you.

Clootie Yeah, maybe. How was your day, plum?

Alex Okay. I had to put my mother's house on the market.

Clootie Shit.

Alex They think I'll get a good price.

Clootie Good.

Alex I need the money to pay for her now.

Clootie 'Course you do.

Alex You disapprove. I know you do.

Clootie No. No, I don't.

Pause.

Alex I don't look like her, you know. There's not one trace of her in my face.

Clootie You look the spit of your dad.

Alex I was always more like him.

Clootie You've done the right thing, Alex. She couldn't look after herself.

Alex She used to cut my fringe. Right up to when I was sixteen or seventeen.

Clootie I wouldn't let her loose with the scissors now if I were you.

Alex No . . . I went to the house today. And she's still there somehow. Giving me little shocks.

Clootie What are those photos?

Alex I found them in her bedside table. I don't know who they are.

Clootie Let's see. Ah! The long lost relatives.

Alex This one's got a name on the back. Livvy Unwin. Thackley, 1908. That's Yorkshire, isn't it? It's more likely to be my dad's family.

Clootie Ask her tomorrow.

Alex Questions tend to freak her out a bit.

Clootie Sometimes they're better with things from ages ago.

Alex Do you think she looks like me? Livvy Unwin? I think she does.

Clootie Maybe. If she had a fringe. She's probably your great-great-aunt and she probably died of diphtheria two weeks after this was taken.

Alex Don't say that.

Clootie How was your mum today?

Alex Aggrieved.

Clootie And how was nurse James?

Alex He asked after you again.

Clootie I love him. He is my prospective saviour.

Alex You should say something to him then.

Clootie I'm too busy raising depression to an art form.

Alex Clootie.

Clootie I might.

Alex I've got to do some work.

Clootie You're so glamorous.

Alex I'm not. You mistake having responsibility for glamour.

Clootie Well I must get on with things too. Cultivate my own bile in a petri dish or some such. Night, night, star.

Alex Sleep well. (*She's still looking at the photos. She sighs*) . . .Livvy Unwin. Livvy. You do look like me. I've got a picture somewhere just like this. We'd gone to Weston-super-Mare! Yes. And there was no sign of the sea. All day the tide had gone out. There was just hundreds of worm casts. I'm staring at the camera, as if to say: 'Where the fuck's the sea? Why have you brought me to this place of worms?' I'm holding a very big spade and a ridiculously small bucket. And I look like you. This one you look nice. Like you're about to say something.

> *Livvy appears behind her during this, watches her. She is beautiful but in an unpredictable way.*

Livvy
My frame was not hidden from you when
I was made in that secret place.
When I was woven together in the depths of the earth,
My eyes saw your unformed body.

Alex Or laugh. Yes, you were about to laugh. What were you laughing at, Livvy Unwin?

Alex gets up and leaves during the next. She is totally unaware of Livvy's presence.

Livvy I can't remember. I can remember that day so clearly. It was beautiful. The best day of my life. But I can't remember the thing that made me laugh. Isn't that funny?

SCENE FOUR

Thackley, 1908.

Clara Livvy! Livvy! Livvy! Livvy! Livvy!

Livvy Clarty-clugs. Where have you been? Gramma's been worried.

Clara I've been on my travels.

Livvy You haven't been listening to walls again?

Gramma enters during this. She is in her early sixties.

Clara No. Well. Only a bit. But Livvy, I met a man. He came right up to me and breathed fire for me. All over me, but I didn't burn.

Gramma Don't tell fibs, child.

Clara I'm not, Gramma.

Gramma Where did you meet this man, Clara? And I want the God's truth.

13

Clara In Reggie Copson's field by the cowshed. Near to where they're setting up Thackley Fair.

Gramma I see. For future reference, I think you'd better steer clear of Reggie Copson's field. And while you're at it you'd best leave men alone especially if they start up any fire-breathing shenanigans. For if a man breathes his fire on you there's no turning back. Now go and help your sister with the tea.

Clara You don't believe me.

Livvy Yes she does. We do believe you, Clara.

Clara I remembered it specially and you don't believe me.

Livvy There now, don't get all worked up, Clara.

Clara No one ever believes me because I'm an idiot.

Gramma Happen I know what occurred in that field today.

Clara What?

Gramma You had an Epiphany.

Clara A what?

Gramma Epiphany.

Clara I don't know about that.

Gramma The Holy Ghost came down on you in Reggie Copson's field.

Clara I don't think so. What does the Holy Ghost look like? Does he have a moustache?

Gramma The Holy Ghost can assume any shape or form.

Clara Is it a good thing if the Holy Ghost comes down on you in a field?

Livvy It's the best thing that could possibly happen. It means you're blessed. It means you'll come to no harm.

Clara That's good, isn't it Gramma?

Gramma No more than you deserve. Now help Livvy with the tea.(*She goes to lie down.*)

Clara Who'd have thought it, Livvy? That I would have an Epiphany in Reggie Copson's field by the cowshed?

Livvy You're a special girl. Come on, we've got raspberries for tea.

Clara runs off followed by Livvy.

SCENE FIVE

The nursing home.

Mother (*getting into bed/chair at nursing home*) Bury me then. Bury me in the sand. Go on. Then you and your dad can run and play in the sea. Ganging up on me. The pair of you. Wasps buzzing about my face. Sand in my crannies. And the radio's gone off the station. Weston-super-bloody-Mare. The donkeys have got mange. Poor fuckers. And I can't move my limbs. I can't move an inch. I don't like it.

Alex enters during the last.

Alex What don't you like, Mother?

Mother Oh. It's you.

Alex Are you tired, Ma? You look tired.

Mother It's terrible here at night.

Alex Is it?

Mother Shouting and wailing. Wandering about like bloody Banshees. Her in there. She just shouts, 'Hurry up,' every few minutes. 'Hurry up, hurry up,' all night. In the end I told her, 'Why don't you hurry up and peg it, you old bat. Give us all some peace.'

Alex And did it shut her up?

Mother Did it, my arse.

Alex Mother.

Mother (*looks at Alex*) You never do what I tell you.

Alex And you never do what I tell you. (*Pause.*) I found these photos in your room. Do you recognise any of them?

Anne looks at them intently, fixes on one.

I thought she looked a bit like me. Livvy Unwin. Is she someone in your family?

Anne knocks them all to the floor except the picture of the girl.

Mother Never seen them before. Ugly fuckers.

Alex You don't have to swear at me, Mother. Let's put them away. Give me that one.

Mother It's mine.

Alex I'll put it with the others. You don't know who they are. Give it back to me.

Mother You stole it from me. Bitch.

Alex All right, Ma. Keep it. It's fine. Keep it.

James enters.

James Here we all are then. How are we doing?

Mother I can smell sulphur.

James Good for you. We like it when Alex comes, don't we Annie?

Alex Anne – her name's Anne.

Mother Annie. Annie. Annie.

Alex All right, that's enough Ma.

James You've been on good form, haven't you? Showing a bit of leg for the lads.

Alex What?

James You were telling us all about your dancing days, weren't you Annie – Anne? We didn't realise we had a dancing queen in our midst.

Alex My mother doesn't dance. You are a fibber, Mother.

Mother What would you know about it?

James It's never too late to learn, is it Annie?

Mother I was magnificent. Gold shoes. Ruffles.

Alex And where was this, Mother? Bromley High Street?

Mother You know nothing about me . . . She's not even married you know.

Alex Here we go.

James Oh, they're all terrible matchmakers in here. All my ladies are worried about me, because I'm on the shelf, isn't that right Annie? They've taken to knitting me a trousseau in the vain hope that I might get hitched one day.

Mother My daughter's a cardigan.

James Is she now?

Alex Cartographer, she means, I think. I'm a cartographer. You know, maps.

James That must be really interesting.

Alex Well, not really. It's all done by computers these days.

Mother Daddy would never use a map.

Alex No that's right, Ma . . . It's a bit of a family joke, that I became a cartographer.

James Yeah?

Mother You got him in the end though, didn't you?

Alex What, Mother?

Mother Don't think I don't know your little games because I do.

Alex That's enough now, Mother.

Mother Had him wrapped round her eye-teeth.

Alex I'm not having a spat with you today, Mother. I'm not in the mood.

Mother Sugar and spice, my arse.

Alex I won't come back if you start this again. Then you'll have no one.

James That's it now, Annie.

Alex Oh it's all right, James. I've got to be going anyway. You can have too much of a good thing. Bye, bye then, Mummy. I'll probably see you tomorrow.

They move away from Anne.

Mother Tuesday's child is full of shit. Hah! I know your games. I can see what's underneath, Missey May.

James Alex?

Alex I have got to be going.

James She doesn't mean it.

Alex Maybe not.

James If you ever want to just –

Alex I'm fine really. Thanks.

James I'm always here. For you too. You know that.

Alex Yes. I know.

James And hi to Clootie.

Alex Sure.

Anne is staring at the photo. All animosity has left her. Alex exits.

James That's a lovely photo, Annie. Who's that pretty lady then?

Mother (*proudly*) That's my daughter.

James Yes, she is pretty, isn't she?

Mother Beautiful. Lovely girl.

James Your daughter.

Mother Yes.

James Do you think she'd fuck me? Your daughter?

Mother I don't see why not. Why don't you ask her nicely, dear?

Thackley, 1908.
   Clara runs on and gets on the bed with Gramma.

Clara Tell me where you found me again, Gramma?

Gramma Washed up on the beach. Flotsam and jetsam. That's what you were. But I thought, 'No. I can take that one home. Find a use for her.'

Clara Are you very wise, Gramma?

Gramma As wise as they come.

Clara I want to be wise like you.

Gramma You have to be very, very old to be wise. Old as Methuselah. You need to have suffered and endured.

Clara Do you think I will be wise one day?

Gramma Sometimes it is better to live in ignorance, Clara. There is no fun involved in being wise. If you want wisdom you must be miserable almost all of the time. I think you will never attain wisdom, Clara. But it is also a blessing to be an idiot and to be happy.

Clara Why do you speak in riddles, Gramma?

Gramma It gives the impression of wisdom, dear child. And it is the prerogative of the aged.

   Livvy enters. Clara stamps her feet.

Clara Livvy!

Livvy Clarabelle!

Gramma That girl will never be a lady if she persists in this incessant stamping.

Clara I like to stamp.

Livvy Perhaps she doesn't want to be a lady.

Gramma You two will be the death of me. Now Livvy, we must decide on a course of happiness for you. Arthur Willis has set his cap at you and I think you could do a lot worse –

Livvy Gramma, Arthur Willis is a calamity.

Gramma Ay, I know right enough what he is. But being a fool has never stopped anyone being a husband.

Clara Arthur Willis got struck by lightning.

Livvy No, it narrowly missed him.

Clara It made his head sizzle.

Livvy He won't make me happy, Gramma.

Gramma There's no point worrying about happy or not happy. Live in a straight line, young lady. I can do no more for you and there's this one to think of. He's got two left feet and a tendency to make horses bolt but he's devoted to you and as long as you keep him away from the mangle, you could muddle through.

Clara Arthur Willis nearly chopped off his thumb.

Livvy Arthur Willis is lucky to have any digits left at all. What if I want more than muddling through with Arthur Willis, Gramma?

Gramma Nothing ever came of wanting more, young lady.

Clara Arthur Willis fell off Minnie Culver's roof.

Gramma Think of your poor mother, Livvy.

Clara Then he had the galloping runs.

Gramma A life of desperate wandering is no life.

Clara (*stops suddenly*) Our mother upped and walked into the sea.

   Pause.

Gramma Hush now, child. Livvy, you could do a lot worse. At least look kindly on the chap. He'd look after you.

Livvy Arthur Willis doesn't do a very good job of looking after himself.

Clara I'm not a child any more.

Gramma No, and I'm an old woman and I can't worry about the pair of you until the day I die.

Livvy All right, Gramma. I'll walk out with him if it will make you happy, but I can't make any promises.

Clara Arthur Willis is very urgent.

Livvy Ay, that he is. Come on, Clarts, let's go and do some stamping.

   Livvy and Clara exit.

SCENE SEVEN

A bar. Mat is sitting at a table, drinking. He is very good-looking, younger than Alex.

Alex I feel sick.

Mat What's up, baby?

Alex I killed a pigeon.

Mat I bet he had it coming to him.

Alex It flew into my windscreen.

Mat There are some fucking kamikaze pigeons about, I tell you.

Alex It was lying on its side staring up at me. I thought it was stunned but it was dead.

Mat Alex. Have you seen the state of some of the pigeons knocking about at the moment? Fuckin' desperate. Pigeons have really let themselves go.

Alex I hate seeing dead things in the road.

Mat Too much compassion can kill you, you know.

Alex (*she smiles*) I know. How's the world of High Finance?

Mat Scintillating. How's the world of Mapmaking?

Alex I've got to do this lecture. 'Mapmaking from the Renaissance to the New Millennium.'

Mat Blimey.

Alex I'm not getting very far.

Mat You'll be great.

Alex I was thinking about you today. How you should have been a Renaissance Man. Eating, drinking and colonising the world. Slaying the fire-breathing dragons.

Mat Nah.

Alex Why not?

Mat They had to wear tights, didn't they?

Alex Oh come on, you're not averse to a bit of Lycra.

Mat I think you have serious fire-breathing tendencies. It's very sexy.

Alex And you want to colonise me?

Mat Yes I do.

Alex Ah, but then you take on responsibilities. You have to cultivate your new-found territory.

Mat But I want my colony to be self-governing.

Alex I don't think you can have it both ways.

Mat Is this a revolt?

Alex No. Not at all.

Mat No one person can give you everything you need.

Alex And what percentage of your needs do I fill?

Mat One hundred per cent. When I'm with you.

Alex And when I'm not with you? You don't think of me at all.

Mat Yes I do. But I control it.

Alex I don't know how you do it. Keep all the parts of your life so airtight. I admire you.

Mat I like to juggle things.

Alex That's what I like about you. You're very slick.

Mat And you give me a run for my money.

Alex Keeping your life in little boxes though. It must get tricky.

Mat I'm a demon at storage, me.

   Alex smiles.

Do you know what I love about you? I never know what you're thinking.

Alex It's a family trait. The one thing my mother taught me. That and invisible mending.

Mat Actually I do think about you quite a lot. You've got under my skin. I didn't mean that to happen.

Alex I know.

Mat How is your mum?

Alex Oh. She's in her favourite place. Occupying the moral high ground.

Mat I love my mum. She taught me everything I know. I can't do wrong in her eyes, but I've told her if she starts to smell I'm bunging her in a home.

Alex Why are you so flippant all the time?

Mat Why are you so serious?

Alex I'm not . . . Maybe I am. Sometimes I wish I could –

Mat What?

Alex I don't know. Splurge. Clootie – the girl I live with. She's in a mess. She's pissing her life up a wall but she makes me feel, I don't know, half-baked sometimes.

Mat I like you the way you are.

Alex But not as much as you like Katherine.

Mat Don't try and catch me out.

Alex I'm not.

Mat I was too young when I got married. It was a mistake.

Alex I have no problem with being the Other Woman. It suits me, Mat. I'm used to it. Ask my mother.

Mat She has been a bit arsey lately, Katherine. I don't know why. She won't talk to me.

Alex Mmm . . . The music here is terrible. It's getting on my nerves.

Mat I like it.

Alex Really?

Mat Yeah. A bit of Latin. I respond to that. Everyone should have a bit of Latin in them. A bit of fire, a bit of passion. Don't deny the Latin in you, Alex.

Alex Must be where I've been going wrong . . . It's my birthday next Thursday. Will you be able to meet me?

Mat You, my darling, are going to be cosseted.

Alex You don't go in for cossetting do you, Mat?

Mat Start getting your hopes up.

SCENE EIGHT

Livvy and Clara.

Clara Livvy, when I'm dead, can I come back and haunt you?

Livvy Don't talk about sad things, Clarty.

Clara It's not always sad to die, Livvy.

Livvy Well, it would be sad for me if you died. Anyway I'm older than you so I shall probably die before you.

Clara But if I do die, can I haunt you, please?

Livvy Why would you want to do that?

Clara Because I would miss you.

Livvy You won't scare me, will you?

Clara No. You won't be able to see me.

Livvy Then how will I know it's you?

Clara (*considers this*) Well I think I will probably stamp a bit. And maybe howl.

Livvy That would be good. Then I'd know for sure it was you and I wouldn't be scared.

Clara Can I practise? How I'm going to haunt you?

Livvy You'd better had. So I can prepare myself.

Clara does a howling and stamping dance. During this Arthur enters and is very shocked by Clara's behaviour. Clara finds this funny.

Arthur You are an evil girl, Clara Unwin, trying to frighten a fellow like that. My heart, Livvy, it's going nineteen to the dozen. I haven't a strong constitution, my mother says. I can't withstand too many more shocks like that. I feel quite faint.

Livvy You'd better sit down, Arthur. Find your breath. Clarty, don't laugh at Arthur. I'd have thought you'd be used to shocks though, Arthur, you've had more than your fair share of them.

Arthur My mother says she's never known anyone more afflicted than me, Livvy. Did you notice I had a slight limp, Livvy, when I arrived?

Livvy I can't say I did, Arthur.

Arthur Yes, indeed, Livvy. I thought it might be polio at first, but no – a blood blister the size of a fist on my foot. It just appeared overnight.

Clara You probably trod on something.

Arthur If I wanted your opinion I'd ask for it.

Livvy You really are afflicted, Arthur.

Arthur Indeed I am. But I have some good news too.

Clara I could burst the blister for you, Arthur.

Livvy That's enough now, Clarty. What's your good news, Arthur?

Arthur I've got myself a good apprenticeship.

Livvy Well, I'm pleased for you, Arthur. Who is it with?

Arthur (*very pleased with himself*) Samuels the butchers.

Livvy Are you sure that's a good idea, Arthur? With your history might it not be better to work somewhere with fewer knives involved? All that chopping, Arthur, are you sure?

Arthur Thank you for your concern, Livvy but mother says I'll be a natural. Which brings me in a roundabout way to what I really wanted to ask you.

Clara I could get Gramma's crochet needle and burst the blood out of it, Arthur.

Arthur What I'm meaning to say, Livvy,, and please hear me out. Bear with me now. Since I'm going to be more in the way of a steady chap, what with my job and everything, I feel it's time to settle down. Stop staring at my foot, Clara Unwin, you can't see it there, it's on the other side anyway – and although my mother says you're a bit flighty, I mean she feels sorry for you on account of first your father and then your mother dying and all, but she thinks that Suki Drivers is a better bet on account of having sturdy hips, but I said to my mother – will you get off my foot – Suki Drivers is a carthorse by compare of Livvy Unwin. I think you'd be a neat wife, not that I'm talking of getting wed yet but I wondered if maybe, you might see your way to – my prospects are good and I love babbies, so I do – what is this damn girl doing clinging to my leg – (*He walks around trying to shake her off.*) – where was I – yes, well the fair is coming to Thackley next week and although last time I did injure myself somewhat on the coconut shy, I'm not a coward and I wondered if you might – GET OFF MY LEG RIGHT NOW YOU IDIOT GIRL – LIKE TO GO WITH ME – whether you might like to, like to go with me?

Pause.

Livvy Pick me up at noon next Saturday. Come on Clarty.

They exit.

Arthur What? Really? Yes. Yes. Noon next Saturday. It's a date. (*He exits.*)

SCENE NINE

Alex and Mat.

Alex I'm binding you. The thread cutting your wrists. I'm going to bind you all over. I'm going to inscribe you with my name. I'm going to lick my name out in your sweat. I'm going to pass my thread through you. I'm going to pull you. I'm going to reel you in. I'm going to well up inside you. I'm going to run through your veins. Till the blood in your veins throb with me. I'm going to breathe inside you. I'm going to ignite you. Kindle you to flame.

Mat I love you, Alex.

Alex smiles.

SCENE TEN

The nursing home. Late at night.
  Anne is slumped over in her chair.

James Annie, you need a bit of a hitch-up, don't you, darlin'?

Mother I can't be bothered.

James Can't be bothered to sit up straight. Dear me, Annie. You have to be able to sit up straight in this life. Didn't your mother teach you that?

Mother All such a bother.

James You need someone to re-charge your batteries, don't you, old girl?

Mother What?

James You need to be handed a new lease of life. You don't want to be old. You want to be brand new, don't you sweetie?

Mother It'll never happen.

James It might, Annie. You see, every seven years your body renews itself. All the cells shift a gear. When you're growing up, you can shoot up an inch overnight. But when you're fully grown it doesn't stop happening, you know. Just the results aren't so easy to notice. We're all renewable, you know.

Mother Oh yes, lovely.

James If you concentrate hard enough, you can feel it inside you. Like your blood suddenly pumps harder. But it only happens every seven years.

Mother That's a shame.

James It is a shame.

   Pause.

But do you know something, Annie? With me, I feel like nothing ever settles. Inside of me is always re-arranging. Sometimes, Annie, the veins in my arms hurt me.

Mother Oh dear. (*Anne starts to inspect her own arm.*)

James It's not a nice feeling.

Mother No.

James Do you understand me, Annie? Perhaps you do. Your brain's all knotted up, isn't it? Can you feel it tangling up? All the memories swelling and swirling about? Can you feel everything that you've lost?

Mother Only on Sundays.

James Yes that's right. On the Sabbath. Pain is always more acute on the Sabbath.

Mother Is this my arm?

James Yes, Annie.

Mother Are you sure?

James Let's have a look. Yes it appears to be your arm, madam. Must have lost its label, that's all.

Mother No sensation.

James I know. Poor Annie. (*He strokes her arm.*)

Mother Not a thing.

James starts to pinch her arm.

James What about now? Do you feel it now?

Mother Dead as a dodo.

He pinches harder.

James What about now?

Mother No. I want an abortion.

James No, no, don't upset yourself. What if I chinese burn it, Annie? No, wait a minute. That's kids' stuff, isn't it, Annie. You want to cry out with the pain, don't you?

Mother Yes.

He gets out a box of matches.

James You've got to concentrate now Annie. I'm going to hurt you now. I'm going to burn you. You're going to

31

feel this. I'm going to singe your skin. I'm going to really, really hurt you. (*He lights a match and holds it up to her arm.*)

Mother (*suddenly alarmed*) You shouldn't play with fireworks.

   Pause.

James No, of course you're right, Annie. But sometimes the temptation is very strong. (*He blows out the flame.*)

Mother I love sparklers.

James Yes. Yes. I bet you do.

Mother Holding the sparklers in my hand. Spinning with the sparklers in my hand.

James We'll have to get you sparklers, then. That's what we'll have to do.

SCENE ELEVEN

Alex's flat.
   Alex enters. Music: Peter Sarstedt, 'Where do you go to my lovely.' Clootie is drinking wine.

Clootie Hi, Alex, how was the married man?

Alex Fine.

Clootie Will I ever meet him?

Alex I don't think so.

Clootie Will he leave his wife?

Alex Eventually. If I want him too. Which I don't.

Clootie You've got it all worked out.

Alex Oh, I've worked long and hard on my mission statement.

Clootie Did you have sex?

Alex Yes. Thank you. How was your evening?

Clootie Oh, much better than yours. I've spent the evening in the company of Peter Sarstedt. He really is thrilling company. He's sung 'Where do you go to, my lovely?' to me twenty-seven times now.

Alex I hate this song. (*She goes and turns the volume down.*)

Clootie So do I. It's a wonder to me that this song was a hit. And do you know what, you never really discover where his lovely does go to – when she's alone in her head. But then again you don't really care either. In fact I defy anyone to like the woman in this song. I don't think she's lovely.

Alex Clootie. Why have you rearranged all the furniture?

Clootie Oh yes. I hope you don't mind. I had an urge to become more south-facing.

Alex Well, if it makes you feel better –

Clootie My mother swears by furniture-moving as therapy. She's feng-shuiing her way towards Paradise. Have we got any paracetamol?

Alex You shouldn't keep taking them.

Clootie I have no immune system. You know that. He robbed me of my immune system.

Alex Not Nigel again, Clootie. Please.

Clootie He took everything, Alex. Even the bloody shower curtains.

Alex I know.

Clootie He only ever has baths.

Alex I know. You're exhausting me, Clootie.

Clootie No, but Alex, I've realised tonight, I am so very nearly over him.

Alex Good.

Clootie I hope he's enjoying wonderful power showers on an hourly basis.

Alex It will get easier, Clootie.

Clootie I can't decide what I find worse though. The fact that he was having sex with other men. Or the fact that he was having it in toilets. What do you think?

Alex I really don't know. Both things are bad.

Clootie Yes, yes they are, aren't they? But the location does make a difference. I wonder if he'd been having sex with another man in – a meadow, say, would I find it any easier to cope with? I find the image of the toilet very troubling, you see.

Alex Yes.

Clootie I imagine the sound of the cistern filling and re-filling and the drip, drip, and the smell, of course. I've got it all in my head in glorious technicolour, Alex. I wish he'd chosen somewhere more aesthetically pleasing.

Alex You have to stop this, Clootie.

Clootie Yes, yes, I do. 'We are hard-pressed on every side but not crushed.'

Alex What?

Clootie St Paul to the Corinthians. I've had him out tonight too. He's very good when you're feeling low, St Paul but not quite as good as Elvis Presley for some reason. Why is it that I still want a boyfriend, Alex? After all this. I don't think I can be fully evolved. I must have some sort of chemical imbalance.

Alex Why don't you ask James out?

Clootie Because I can't. I haven't got the necessary – what-do-you-call-it.

Alex But you like him.

Clootie Yes. I do. A lot.

Alex He's lovely. He cares for old people. He's nice-looking but –

Clootie – but not totally out of my league, I know.

Alex I didn't mean that.

Clootie But I can't imagine asking him out, Alex. I can imagine say waking from a coma and finding him right there holding my hand, but I can't ask him out. It's humiliating. He'll say no. He'll probably howl in derision at me.

Alex Of course he won't. He likes you. He laughs at all your jokes. He always asks after you. You should get your wonderbra on and get down there.

Clootie You don't understand, Alex, I'm not like you, the prospect of happiness renders me utterly paraplegic. I'm a Catholic. I've been brought up never to expect anything good.

Alex You're being ridiculous, Clootie. It's a match made in Catholic heaven. Now why don't you come with me tomorrow?

Clootie I don't think so.

Alex Well, just to see my mum then. My mum would like to see you. And it would take the pressure off me.

Clootie It would be nice to see her.

Alex She always really liked you. 'Clootie always says thank you.'

Clootie Yes, well, I was brought up to be grateful.

Alex That's settled then. I'm looking forward to it. (*She goes and switches off the record.*)

SCENE TWELVE

Thackley, 1908.
   Arthur and Livvy process on with Gramma close behind.

Arthur I didn't know as Gramma Unwin would be coming with us to the fair, Livvy.

Livvy Gramma wouldn't let me come unchaperoned to the fair with an urgent young man like you, Arthur.

Gramma What's he saying?

Arthur Nothing . . .We haven't seen you at Samuels the Butchers this week, Gramma Unwin.

Gramma No, well I wanted to make sure you had all your fingers, Arthur, before I go buying any more of their pork sausages. Now and don't you be getting too close to that young girl. And while we're at it, if you've any sharp objects in your pockets you'd better be giving them to me now. We don't want this day ending in tears.

Livvy Leave him be, now Gramma.

Gramma I shall walk behind you two. But I'm watching you, Arthur, so no funny business with my grandchild.

Arthur No, Gramma Unwin.

Clara enters.

(*sotto voce*) Not the idiot girl as well.

Livvy Don't call her that.

Clara Will you take me on all the rides, Arthur?

Livvy Don't be pestering Arthur now, Clarty.

Arthur I can go on no rides with you, Clara, for I have a queasy stomach.

Clara Arthur Willis will never make anyone happy.

Gramma Come with me now, Clara and we'll find a use for you. Remember what I said now, Arthur Willis.

Arthur You've nothing to worry about with me, Gramma Unwin. Livvy is safe in my hands.

Gramma and Clara exit.

Livvy Well.

Arthur You look very beautiful, Livvy.

Livvy Thank you, Arthur.

Arthur What would you like to do? I've got my first week's wages with me, Livvy, and I don't mind telling you I intend to spend at least a third on you. So name it, Livvy. Anything.

Livvy I don't mind, Arthur.

Arthur Can I kiss you then, Livvy?

Livvy Why don't we wander about a bit first, Arthur, take in the sights.

Arthur Whatever you want, Livvy. This is your day. But I am hoping you'll see your way to letting me kiss you at some stage of the proceedings, Livvy. I've talked to me mates and they said it's not too much to ask of you now that we're officially courting. I wouldn't have said anything but I'd have just worried the whole time about it, when to make a move and so forth and Mother says it's better to get things out in the open if they're on your mind. So any time you want me to kiss you just say the word, Livvy. I'll be ready for you.

Livvy Thank you, Arthur. I'll bear that in mind.

Frank enters, as Fabrizio, with a camera on a tripod. As he speaks he sets up the camera.

Fabrizio Buon giorno! Ah bella bella Signorita! The Great Fabrizio at your service. Take my card. (*Looks at card.*) No. No. Wrong card. Scusa.

Arthur No thank you.

Fabrizio I am here, madonna, for one night only. Sad news, I know. No please. It is all I can do. One night. For you at the most a week. Then back to Verona. No tears, please. I cannot stand to see the ladies cry.

Arthur She's not crying.

Fabrizio For now I am at your convenience. I will do all I can do for you, madonna.

Arthur We don't want anything, thank you very much.

Livvy Arthur.

Fabrizio Please sir. I must ask you to hold your horses. Please. Rein them in. Two minutes of your time is all I ask. Madonna, here you see the humble box that is the tool of my trade. With this I capture the present. Poof! Beautiful, no? I give you something to remember for the rest of your life. A whisper of happy times. My life's duty is to capture rare moments of beauty. Life is hard, yes? But there are moments, wonderful moments, eh madonna?

Livvy Yes.

Arthur How much for one photograph?

Fabrizio All I ask is uno, duo, tres, quattro, half a crown. Half a crown! Look at this woman, sir. Look at her. You are a lucky man. Shake my hand. Shake it. (*Arthur does.*) Later I buy you a pint. She is a rare creature. I should know. I have travelled the world. I have seen beauty, oh yes I have, I have been to the Far Indies and seen the birds of paradise. I have held them in my hand, the most fantastico creatures in this world. See? I weep as I remember. What do you say, Arthur? Half a crown only for a photograph of this beautiful lady?

Livvy is laughing.

Arthur Come on now.

Fabrizio Oh, lady, pretty lady. You don't wanna walk away from me, huh. It will break my heart if I cannot photograph you. For you, I will waive my fee. Only one shilling for I must capture you with my humble box. What's your name, pretty lady? No, don't tell me. I guess.

Arthur That's it, we're going.

Fabrizio Vittoria? No. Emilia? No. Don' tell me, now. I am a magician. I can see inside your head. Beatrice? No. Jane? No. Of course not. I insult you with such a name. There, see, I smite myself for such ignorance. I have it, I have it, Lucia! No. Consumpta? No –

Arthur Livvy. Come on, now.

Fabrizio LIVVY! LIVVY! Of course. I knew it. Livvy. Perfecto. Livvy – lives. Livvy – full of life. Perfect.

Arthur We're leaving now, thank you very much, erm, er –

Fabrizio I am the Great Fabrizio of Florenza, at your service Arthur.

Arthur Well, Great Fabrizio. Look here, old chap, it's very kind of you but we won't be requiring your services –

Livvy No, Arthur. Get Gramma and Clara. I'd like a photograph of us all.

Arthur But Livvy –

Livvy You said this was my day. And it'll be a nice memento for us. Please, Arthur. Go and get them. I'll wait here. Quickly.

Fabrizio My advice to you, Arthur. Always do what the women say. It make your life much easier. Take it from one who knows.

Arthur Very well. Will you be all right?

Livvy Of course.

Arthur Well, I shall run, which I don't mind telling you is something my mother told me to avoid at all costs.

Livvy I'll be waiting.

   Arthur exits.

Livvy Where will I stand, for the photograph?

Fabrizio Permit me to show you, madonna. You are a true beauty, if I may say so. Like the female bird of paradise.

Livvy I thought the female birds of paradise were very dowdy. It's the male birds that are beautiful.

Fabrizio Indeed, you are right.

Livvy The male birds have resplendent tail and head feathers, of azure and gold and vermilion but they only display them when they want to win a mate.

Fabrizio You know a great deal about them.

Livvy I read a lot. I would like more than anything to travel.

Fabrizio I have been to the farthest corners of the globe.

Livvy It must be a real comedown to have to photograph at Thackley Fair.

Fabrizio Not when Thackley has such a bird of paradise.

Livvy And when the birds of paradise show their plumage they also dance for their mate, don't they? While she looks on.

Fabrizio That's right.

Livvy And you have seen them.

Fabrizio Of course. I will remember that dance until the day I die.

Livvy Show me.

Fabrizio What?

Livvy Show me how they dance.

Fabrizio You want me to show you how they dance.

Livvy Yes. Just roughly. To give me some idea.

Fabrizio Of course. For you, I will do this . . . (*He is improvising.*) First of all they let down their tail feathers, a wiggle, thus. Then they mark out their territory, backward, forward motion, thus. Then they display their head feathers. Then they begin to vibrate. Side to side. Up and down. An orgy of colour. But they do not look at their mate once. No, they are proud fellows. Then the dance begins.

> *Fabrizio does a funny, strange, jerky dance with mad head movements and strange throat noises. Livvy watches amused.*

Fabrizio That is more or less it.

Livvy That was very illuminating. Your name isn't Fabrizio is it?

He shakes his head.

Livvy What is it?

Fabrizio (*he drops the Italian accent*) Frank.

Livvy And you're not from Verona or Florence, are you?

Frank I'm from Skipton.

Livvy And you haven't travelled to the far-flung corners of the globe.

Frank I've never been outside Yorkshire.

Livvy And you've never seen a bird of paradise have you, Frank?

Frank Not till today.

Clara enters.

Livvy Here she is. This is Clara.

Frank (*slight falter*) Clara? And I am the Great Fabrizio. Can I give you my card?

Clara I know you.

Frank I don't think so, signorita.

Livvy Have you been on the rides, Clarty?

Clara No. I've been listening to the walls. There's some pretty good walls here.

Livvy Clara, we didn't bring you to the fair so you could listen to walls.

Frank If she wanna listen to the walls, she should listen to the walls.

Clara Yes Livvy. I'm sure I know you.

Livvy He's only just come to Thackley, Clara. The Great Fabrizio only makes very brief forays into the public eye.

Frank This is correct. What you say. Is correct.

Clara Can you keep secrets?

Frank Can I keep secrets! She wanna know, if I, the Great Fabrizio can keep secrets! Come here. I am world renowned for my secret-keeping ability. Any secret you tell me will go no further than between you, me and the goalpost. Even if I travel the world I will not breathe a word. I would rather have my hands cut off than tell your secret. No I would die first.

Livvy You don't have any secrets, Clarty-Clugs.

Clara Of course I do. You can't live and be a lady unless you have a secret to tell.

Frank What she says – it is true. I think you are very wise.

Clara (*delighted*) Am I?

Frank If I tell you this, it is true.

Clara I'm going to tell you my best secret.

Livvy Clara.

Frank No, no, is too much. Too great an honour. Even I, the Great Fabrizio, must sometimes know when to draw the line.

Clara No, please.

Frank I don't know if my heart can stand it.

Clara Livvy, please turn your back.

Frank Yes. This is a necessary precaution.

Clara Go further off. Now.

Livvy All right, Clara.

Frank Please to whisper. For security reasons it is always best to whisper secrets.

Clara (*with pointed look at Livvy*) Good idea. (*She whispers in his ear.*)

Frank Perhaps I think a little bit louder.

Clara whispers again – a stage whisper.

Clara I had an Epiphany in Reggie Copson's field by the cowshed.

Frank Yes, yes. I knew it. I could tell at a glance. There now, your secret is safe.

Clara I hope I can trust you.

Frank It is etched on my heart. A special moment has passed between us, no?

Clara We're friends now because you know my secret.

Frank And what about Livvy? Do you think she will share a secret with me?

Clara I think you've got enough to do with safeguarding my secret.

Livvy I don't have any secrets.

Frank I don't think that is true.

Clara She's certainly not as good as me at having secrets, Great Fabrizio.

Frank No, she is very bad at secrets, Livvy, you know why? Because her heart is in her face.

Arthur and Gramma enter.

Arthur She's here all the time. Clara Unwin, we've been high and low for you.

Frank Ah! Scusa, scusa ladies, we must prepare for the big moment. If I can just move you over here. And you, madam, what may I call you?

Gramma You can call me what you like. And there's no need to manhandle me. I don't hold with foreigners I'll tell you now, and Arthur was right about you, but I should like to have a photograph so let's get this over and done with.

Frank I defer to you, great, wise lady.

Arthur Where shall I stand? Next to Livvy?

Frank As you wish. Now everybody, a big smile for the Great Fabrizio.

Gramma I'm not going to smile.

Clara Can I stamp?

Livvy No, you must be still, Clarty.

Frank Yes, Arthur, great gusto, but you are obscuring the lovely Livvy.

Arthur Less of the lovely, from you. I'm paying for this.

Frank (*he looks at Livvy*) No, I ask no fee. This is a pleasure for me.
    And ready?

Flash

Yes. Very good. Perhaps a little less fierce this time from the great lady.

During this dialogue Frank takes photos.

Livvy Don't scowl, Gramma.

Gramma I'll 'ave you know I'm troubled with wind.

Arthur I suffer terrible from wind. My mother says I was born with a twisted colon.

Flash.

Clara Can I see it, Arthur?

Livvy It's on the inside, Clara.

Arthur I was a breach baby. I didn't breathe for a good minute when I was born. I was purple for the first week of my life.

Gramma It's a wonder they didn't put you out of your misery straight off.

Flash

Clara You're still a funny colour, Arthur.

Livvy He's not a funny colour, Clara.

Gramma He's sallow. All the Willises are sallow.

Frank Arthur, can you smile?

Arthur I'm beginning to feel very unwell.

Gramma Dose of salts is what I would recommend for you, Arthur Willis.

Flash.

Clara You can kill someone with salt.

Arthur Can you?

Clara Yes. It's called salt killing. Can I have one on my own?

Gramma Vanity is a terrible sin, Clara Unwin.

Livvy No, let her, Gramma.

Arthur I need to put my head between my legs.

Gramma Yes, best place for it, lad.

Frank All the ladies I take on their own, yes?

Gramma I bet you do.

Clara Me first.

Frank Beautiful. The camera loves you. There is something very noble in your brow, Clara. Smile for me. With all your teeth. Good girl.

Flash.

Clara I think I love the Great Fabrizio.

Gramma Come and sit here, before your heart takes flight all together now, Clara.

Clara Was I beautiful, Gramma?

Gramma From the day you were born.

Frank And you, madonna?

Gramma No, I don't want my face out wandering the world without my people beside me. I think that's us done.

Arthur Yes, we should be heading off now.

Clara What about Livvy?

Gramma She's not bothered, are you?

Arthur We could get saveloy and chips, Livvy.

Clara Yes please.

Livvy I thought you had a queasy stomach, Arthur.

Arthur Must be hungry, that's all. I've a very fast metabolism, my mother says.

Gramma Come on then. Let's be having you.

Frank No! Please. I will take the lady's picture. Please. I have only a few pictures left. I must finish them today.

Arthur It's getting dark.

Frank But Livvy has her own light. Please, Livvy, permit me?

Clara Say cheese, Livvy!

Frank No, say, formaggio!

Gramma She's not saying filth. If she says anything it will be the Lord's word.

Clara Livvy has all the psalms by heart. She says them to me till I fall asleep.

Gramma Ay, that's it, Livvy. Give us a psalm. (*pointedly at Frank*) There's evil all around.

Livvy (*intently to Frank who stops looking through the camera lens to watch her*)
I praise you because I am fearfully and wonderfully
   made,
Your works are wonderful, I know that full well.
My frame was not hidden from you when I was made
   in that secret place,
When I was woven together in the depths of the earth,
Your eyes saw my unformed body

Arthur Are you sure that's from the Bible?

Clara He's forgotten to take the picture. The Great Fabrizio forgot to take the picture.

Gramma It's the Lord's word, all right.

Livvy You didn't take my picture.

Clara Livvy went all shimmery. Did you see her? She went all shimmery.

Arthur I'm going for my saveloy and chips.

Frank (*from now on Frank drops his Italian accent*) Yes, she did.

Gramma Hold your horses, Arthur, you can buy me a skate and chips. I might even stretch to a pickled egg.

Arthur Are you coming, Livvy?

Livvy I'll be right there.

Gramma You can take my arm, Arthur Willis. I'm fit to drop.

Arthur Do you think my arms are the same length Gramma Unwin?

Gramma You've enough deformities to sink a thousand ships, Arthur Willis. Now let's be off.

Arthur All right, all right. Livvy?

Livvy I'm right behind.

Gramma and Arthur exit.

Livvy You didn't take the picture.

Clara You were full of fizz, Livvy.

Frank I didn't need to take the picture.

Clara Sparks flew off you, Livvy.

Livvy But I want something to remember.

Clara You went like a sherbert dip in my mouth.

Frank You will remember.

Livvy Take it anyway.

Clara I want to go fizzy too.

Frank Smile then.

Clara (*starts to spin on the spot*) Look! I'm spinning. Am I going fizzy?

Livvy I don't want to smile.

Clara (*spinning*) I'm whizzing and whizzing in the sky.

Livvy I want to laugh.

Clara Look at me, Great Fabrizio! Look at me!

Frank At whose beauty the Sun and Moon stand amazed.

Clara I can shimmer too!

Livvy I want to laugh! I want to laugh!

Livvy and Clara are both laughing, Clara spinning round and round on the spot. Frank takes Livvy's picture. Blackout.
Interval.

Act Two

SCENE ONE

The nursing home.

James Who's been a naughty girl, then?

Mother Stop manhandling me.

James Thinking of emigrating, were you?

Alex What's wrong?

James Annie's been on a walkabout.

Mother I went to the fair.

Alex No you didn't, Mother.

Mother How do you know? I went to the fair on a motorbike.

James It's all right. A lot of them go wandering at night. She didn't come to any harm. Did you, Annie?

Alex Why did you go wandering off, Mother?

Mother I've lost something. I just can't find it.

Alex What is it? Tell me. What have you lost?

Mother (*agitated*) I don't know. I don't know.

James Don't worry, Annie. Let's sit you down.

Alex It's all right, Mum, I'm here. You don't have to worry.

Mother (*she looks at James*) He tried to burn me. I was very very scared.

James No need to worry now, Annie. You're safe. You're safe now Alex is here.

Mother (*looks at her for the first time. With pleasure*) Alex!

Clootie enters.

Alex Yes and look who's come too!

Anne looks confused.

Clootie Hello Anne. Don't you look well.

She kisses her.

Alex Annie. Apparently she prefers Annie now.

Clootie Ah. Annie. All right, Annie? Hi, James.

James Clootie. Lovely to see you again.

Mother Who are you?

Alex Mum, don't be silly. It's Clootie.

Mother Who?

Alex Clootie.

Mother Suzy?

Clootie No. Clootie.

Mother Ruby?

Alex Clootie. Clootie. Her name's Clootie.

Mother Clootie? What sort of name is that?

Clootie A bloody stupid name, Annie.

James It's a nice name.

Mother Clootie? No.

Alex We were at school together, Ma.

Clootie I was named after a cake.

James No!

Mother Alex?

Clootie My mother's idea.

Alex What, Ma?

James What kind of cake?

Mother Who's Annie?

Clootie A clootie dumpling.

Alex You are, Ma.

Clootie A suet and raison dumpling.

Mother Oh fuck it.

Clootie My sentiments exactly.

Alex Clootie's a great name. It's better than Alex. Alex is too hard.

Clootie Clootie MacBride. I mean my parents seriously disliked me.

James You could have been a very successful folk singer.

Alex Clootie's a lovely name.

James Alex suits you. It's not hard, I mean, you're not at all hard.

Clootie Yes, I can see it now. Clootie MacBride and the Dumplings. I shall wear a kaftan, and play the harp and sing songs of lost love and lost hair.

James Are your parents Scottish?

Mother Lost.

Clootie No. They're from Tunbridge Wells.

Mother Lost.

James Oh.

Alex All right, Ma.

Mother I wish I was young. My whole life ahead of me. (*She starts to cry.*)

Alex Don't cry, Ma. Please. I hate it when you cry.

Clootie You don't want to be young, Annie. Being young is rubbish.

Alex We're not young any more. We're in our thirties.

Mother I used to be brand new.

Alex I've got a photo of my mum on her honeymoon and she looks like Audrey Hepburn. Don't you, Ma?

James She's still a stunner, aren't you, Annie? Sets all our hearts fluttering.

Clootie Oh God, sorry, Annie these are for you. (*She hands her a bunch of flowers.*)

Mother I can't abide carnations.

Alex They're chrysanthemums, Mother.

Mother I wanted wild flowers.

James These are very pretty, Annie.

Mother Snapdragons. Hollyhocks. Poppies. And cornflowers. And lots of fern. It stretched nearly to the ground.

Clootie What did, Annie?

Mother It was too heavy to carry. Over ten pounds. It was a burden really. My dad helped me carry it up the aisle. Then I handed it to Margery Evans. She nearly buckled under the weight.

Clootie Ah, your wedding bouquet. How lovely.

Mother Margery Evans was a scrawny bint, though. She became a nun not long after. Only life she was fit for.

Alex Mother, I think you're making this up.

Mother I couldn't throw it. They always want you to throw it. I couldn't, it was too heavy. I wanted it wild though.

James Shall I take those, Annie?

Alex Mother, you're such a terrible fibber. I've got her wedding photos. You had a posy, didn't you?

Mother How do you know? You weren't there. You don't know anything about me.

James I'll put them in a nice vase for you.

Clootie No, we can do it.

James No, no, it's one of my main accomplishments. Hours of training at nursing school. Back in a tick. (*James exits.*)

Mother (*to Clootie*) It was because of her, you see.

Clootie Was it?

Mother I had to have a long one. She was already quickening inside me. I had to cover her up. You can't let on about the quickening.

Alex (*pointedly*) Clootie?

Clootie I can't do it.

Mother What?

Alex Yes you can. For God's sake, Clootie. He really likes you. He laughs at everything you say.

Mother It's all a leap in the dark, dear. You spend your whole life leaping.

Clootie He is so nice. He's devoted his life to old people. He must be gay.

Mother So very, very dark.

Alex (*exasperated*) Clootie.

Mother Can't see a bloody thing.

Clootie We hate homosexuals, don't we, Annie? They should be bludgeoned.

Mother Yes, dear. *if anyone's still up ; laugh More.*

Alex Clootie.

Mother And vegetarians.

Clootie He's coming back.

Alex Do it.

James enters with the vase of flowers.

James There we go then.

Alex Don't they look lovely?

Mother Lovely. Are they mine? Who are they from?

Clootie They're from me, Annie.

Mother Who are you?

Clootie Oh dear. I feel a bit of a conversation loop coming on. I'd better be going. Bye, Annie. God bless.

Alex Clootie?

James Well, we'll see you again, Clootie.

Clootie Yep.

James Bye then.

Clootie Bye. (*She goes to exit, turns.*) I hope you don't mind me asking, James.

James What?

Clootie Do you like tapas?

James Sorry?

Clootie Tapas. You know. Spanish. Food. On plates. I just love tapas.

James Oh.

Mother Tapas.

Clootie Do you?

James What?

Mother Tap. Tap. Tap.

Clootie Like Tapas?

James Yeah, I don't mind.

Clootie There's a new place opened on King Street. Do you want to go? Next Thursday? Maybe?

Alex I've heard it's really good.

James Oh. Thursday. Sure. Why not? I'm working the night shift but I don't need to be here till midnight.

Clootie Great. Shall we meet there about seven?

Mother I know what I lost.

Alex Do you, Mum?

James Whatever. Yeah. Great. Are you coming, Alex?

Alex I'm not sure yet.

Clootie But we could go anyway?

Mother Tap.

James Why not?

Mother Tap shoes. I lost my tap shoes.

Clootie What?

James Annie's a little Cyd Charisse.

Clootie So that's a date?

Alex (*laughing*) No she's not.

Mother Will you find me my tap shoes dear?

Clootie Yes?

Alex Yes.

James Yes.

Mother That's good.

   Blackout.

SCENE TWO

Thackley, 1908.
  Frank and Livvy.

Frank I've thought about you all week.

Livvy I know.

Frank Livvy.

Livvy Show me your hand, Frank.

Frank Why?

Livvy I'm going to read your future.

Frank You can do that?

Livvy Oh yes. Didn't I tell you, I've got mystical powers?

Frank It doesn't surprise me.

Livvy Let's see. (*She takes his hand.*) Oh dear.

Frank What?

Livvy I see itchy feet.

Frank Where?

Livvy It's written all over your palm. Itchy feet.

Frank You're wrong.

Livvy I see paths leading you away.

Frank Where to?

Livvy Far-flung places.

Frank How far-flung?

Livvy Very. The furthest-flung you can get.

Frank I'll take you with me. Where do you want to go?

Livvy I want to go everywhere.

Frank What does it say in my hand? Where are we going to go?

Livvy The road leads you north. To the sea.

Frank That'll be Scarborough. Yes. Do you fancy a trip to Scarborough?

Livvy No, I don't think it's Scarborough. More exotic than Scarborough.

Frank Whitby then. Filey at a push. No, let's have a look, I think it's definitely Whitby.

Livvy laughs.

Livvy It could be Whitby.

Frank Wait a minute. (*He smells his hand.*) I can smell kippers. Smoked kippers. It must be Whitby. Smell.

Livvy Mmm. Definitely something fishy.

Frank That's it then.

Livvy I don't think you're taking me with you.

Frank Of course I am.

Clara enters.

Livvy Clara!

Frank (*Italian accent*) Hello, Princess.

Clara Great Fabrizio! I've found some new walls. I thought maybe we could go and listen to them together.

Frank Of course! But first I've got some pictures here and there's a certain princess in them who looks very, very beautiful.

Clara Is that me?

Frank I don't know any other princesses. Now I'll give them to you but you must look at them very quietly. No stamping. Because if you're too noisy when you look at photographs they start to disappear. And we wouldn't want that, would we?

Clara No.

Frank Sit a little way off.

Livvy Where we can see you, Clarty.

Clara (*a little reluctantly*) All right. But we can go and listen to some walls later?

Frank My ears are itching for some walls, princess.

She takes the photos and sits down and looks at them.

Frank (*to Livvy*) Now let me do you. No, not your hand. Hands are for beginners. I like to chart the whole person. Stand there that's it. Be still. Now let's see. (*He* *moves around her slowly. He never actually touches her though.*) We'll just do from the waist upwards. From the equator. This will tell us all we need to know. We don't need to stray down into the tropics. Not today anyway.

Livvy Frank!

Frank This is our first continent. Your back. Oh yes. This is a beautiful place but largely undiscovered. This is, tell me where –

Livvy Asia.

Frank Yes, Asia. And down the vertebrae. Into the arch of your back. The small of your back. This is a frightened place. A little island.

Livvy Timor Island.

Frank Yes. Look at these. I love these. The hairs on your forearms. Up through the grasslands. The pampas. Oh. This is a smooth warm place. Your belly. This is –

Livvy Italy?

Frank More exotic.

Livvy Brazil?

Frank Perfect. And upwards. It's getting very hot now.

Livvy Frank, I'm watching you.

Frank This bit is definitely South America. I've always wanted to go to South America.

Livvy It's too far. And it's a dangerous place. Unpredictable.

Frank I'm definitely going there one day though. But for now I shall lose myself here. Your face. Your face is like the whole world. No, the sun. You see. You turn, and I can only orbit round you.

He turns her around as if she were a globe while he moves slowly round her.

I want to hold the sun in my hands.

Livvy You want to eclipse me?

Frank No, I'm definitely a sun worshipper. (*He pulls her into him.*) Livvy, I don't need to travel the world.

Livvy But you promised me kippers.

Frank I'll just pop to Whitby then. But I'll come straight back.

Livvy All right then.

They are about to kiss. During the last Clara has stopped looking at the photos. She watches Livvy and Frank. Then she gets up.

Clara I'm not beautiful. You lied to me. I'm not beautiful like Livvy. I'm ugly. I can see that in the pictures. And you're not the Great Fabrizio. Your name is Frank. And I have met you before. You said we'd never met, but you came and breathed your fire on me and now you only want to breathe your fire on her. And I told you my secret and now you only want to hear her secrets. I hate you. I hate you both. You both lied to me.

Livvy Clara. No. You are beautiful. I'm sorry.

Clara I'm the idiot girl. And I'm ugly. See. Look at the photos. He's made me look ugly. I hate you, Livvy. (*She throws the photos down and runs out.*)

Livvy No wait. Please, Clarty. I'm sorry. Please wait. Frank, I'm sorry. I'll have to go after her.

Frank No, Livvy. Don't go.

Livvy But I have to see if she's all right.

Frank She'll be all right. Come here. Please. They all ask too much of you. I want to look after you.

Livvy I don't know.

Frank Hush. Don't speak. This is our time. I love you, Livvy. Do you love me too? Please Livvy.

Livvy Yes. Yes. I do.

He kisses her tenderly.

SCENE THREE

The nursing home.

Alex Here we are then, Mother. (*She gets the tap shoes out and places them before her.*) Nothing to hold you back now. And I've brought you another treat. Raspberry Royale. That's what you wanted, isn't it? They had Sherry Trifle too but you turned your nose up at that last time. Ah. We're going for the silent treatment, are we? (*Pause. The next is very chatty, light, conversational.*) Well. It's my birthday today. I didn't get your card. Second post, maybe. Thirty-six today. I don't look it? Thank you very much. I use extremely expensive eye cream. Guaranteed to cover that 'not-quite-as-fertile-as-I-used-to-be-look' that's creeping up under my eyes. Anyway, I'm meeting Mat later. Did I tell you about him? I don't think you'd approve. He's an acquired taste. And he's married. I fell right into that cliché. Very good in bed though. We get up to all sorts. Your mind, if you had one, would boggle. He never holds my feet though . . .

Pause.

Come on, tuck in. Can't let a good Raspberry Royale go to waste. Raspberries fit for a queen. Come on. You don't have to watch your figure any more. Open wide and let the choo-choo train in. (*Pause. The tone is sharper suddenly.*) Eat up, mother. It's a treat. Come on.(*She feeds her during the next.*) Oh dear, it's all down your front, Mother. You look a right old mess, don't you? (*She looks at her.*) You're very quiet today. Now you haven't got your audience.

Livvy enters.

But I can see you're thinking. It's all going on in there, isn't it? Pickfords must have been, Mother. The careful movers. Packed you away with the crocks and the glassware. But it's all right because I know what you're thinking. Slugs leave trails, you see.

Livvy No.

Alex comes right up close to her.

Alex I was a little girl. You were the one who turned it into a competition. I was just a little girl. Sweetness and light, my arse. You play dirty, don't you, Anne?

Livvy Tell her.

Alex Well it doesn't matter. He's dead now. My dad's dead. I still dream about him though. It's a recurring dream. We're at Weston-super-Mare and we're burying you in the sand. And then we just leave you. We run off together and we have ice-cream. Neopolitan flavour, because I can never choose. And I wake up and I feel safe and then I realise that we've forgotten you, you're still there buried in the sand and I feel guilty for the rest of the day.

Livvy She knows but tell her anyway.

Alex What's so ironic, what you don't realise, Ma, is I still want to help you. I'm here with my spade. And I'm ready to dig.

Livvy Good.

Alex But you're not interested are you?

Livvy It's nearly time.

Alex Just answer me one thing, Mother, why does this feel like a punishment? You being ill, and helpless. Tell me what I've done. Come on. (*Alex sighs.*) Well, you win. (*As an afterthought she kisses her on the head.*)

>   She leaves.
>   During the next Anne has great difficulty speaking.

Livvy Put your shoes on then. Here, let me give you a hand.

Mother Th–, th–, th– THANK you, d–, d–, dear.

Livvy They look lovely.

Mother You're a g–, g–good girl, Alex. But your fr–, fr–, fr–fringe needs c–cut–cutting.

Livvy Are you ready?

Mother Just about.

>   She gets up with great effort. Her one arm is senseless as if she's had another stroke. They go to leave. An afterthought.

Mother You know I l–, l–, l–, l–, love you, Alex, don't you?

Livvy Yes, of course.

>   They go to exit. Anne's movement is very laboured. Anne exits.

SCENE FOUR

Frank enters. He laboriously composes his letter.
  Livvy lingers to listen to him. Perhaps she takes out a letter and reads it as he speaks.

Frank Dear Livvy, Sorry for my delay in writing to you. By the time you read this letter, I will be gone. No. Long gone.
  Forgive me. I'm not very good at goodbyes.
  You were right. I'm off on my travels again. I don't know where. Further than Yorkshire this time I hope. Ha. Ha.
  I won't forget you.
  I'm sorry Livvy. I never meant to be more than what I seemed. Does that make sense? No.
  I never meant to get your hopes up. Better.
  I'm a bad sort all together and you're better shot of me. Regards to your family. Take care of yourself.
                    Yours, etcetera,
                    The Great Lorenzo.
  P.S. I got tired of Fabrizio. The great Lorenzo has got a real ring to it, don't you think?

  He exits.

Livvy Frank? But we haven't picked a name yet. I wanted us to pick the name together.

  She sinks down.

Thackley, 1908.
  Livvy sits silently. Gramma and Arthur stand around her.

Gramma You foolish, foolish girl. You've thrown your life away. And where is he? Vanished into thin air. Well, I can do no more for you now. I've done my best for you for your poor mother's sake. But no more. And what have you to say for yourself? No, it's as well you're silent. For we don't want to hear what you have to say. As for Clara, I don't know what you've done to her but you've broken that poor simple girl's heart.

Arthur That's enough now, Gramma Unwin.

Gramma Ay, I shan't waste my words on her. For she's surely lost. What were you thinking of, girl? To let the first chap that comes along turn your head. And don't think, madam, that I don't know who it was, for I do.

Arthur Who was it, Livvy?

Gramma No, we shan't speak of him, Arthur. Not in this house. With his fancy words.

Arthur Was it –

Gramma No, Arthur, don't speak of it.

Arthur But I reckon –

Gramma Arthur, be silent.

Arthur But I only want to –

Gramma Arthur, I've warned you.

Arthur But can I just –

Gramma Arthur I must beg of you to hold your tongue.

Arthur No, I don't want to know who –

Gramma Are you a complete fool, Arthur Willis? Hush up. We won't speak of what's past . . . Now my girl, Arthur here has something to say to you and you'll listen hard to what he has to say and you'll be grateful for what he has to say for I wouldn't be saying what he is saying if I were in his place but he's told me he wants to say it and I cannot stop him although you don't deserve such good treatment, so listen up hard and good, young lady, to what he has to say and don't say anything till he's said it.

   Slight pause.

For God's sake speak up, Arthur Willis, for the suspense is killing us.

Arthur Oh sorry, Gramma Unwin, am I to speak now?

Gramma Of course you're to speak if you still have something to say.

Arthur Livvy, I –

Gramma Not that she deserves to be called by her own name.

Arthur Livvy, I know as the baby's not mine –

Gramma No, that baby is lost before it's born.

Arthur And I know as you maybe don't love me.

Gramma She's in no position to love or not love.

Arthur And I know as we never really got started.

Gramma She was too busy getting started elsewhere. And look where getting started got you, young lady. You should have stopped getting started before getting started stopped you.

Arthur ENOUGH! Gramma Unwin. I must speak and you must be silent.

Gramma There's no need to get uppity with me, Arthur.

Arthur I'm not getting uppity, Gramma Unwin, but nothing will stop me from saying what I have to say. My mother says I shouldn't, Livvy, that I will bring shame upon my own head, but I'll still have you. Ay, and bring up this baby as my own. I'll stand by you and look after you, Livvy, and all I ask is you stand by me, too.

Gramma And you can't say fairer than that, young lady. And it's more than you deserve.

Arthur ignores her and takes Livvy's hand.

Arthur I know I'm a fool, Livvy. But with you I think I could learn to be wise. I love you, Livvy. I love you till I'm fit to burst. And then I love you still more. You don't have to say anything. Just a nod, a look, Livvy to say you'll be mine.

Silence.

Gramma (*quietly*) Ay, come on lad, you've said it. Now we must leave her be.

They exit.

Livvy You are not lost, child. You will always know who your mother is. I'm saving up my words for you. You shall have a different story every day, child, so that you will be born wise and full of memory. You will have an extraordinary pair of lungs. You will chatter all day and all night and no one will ever tell you to be quiet. (*She touches her stomach. Quietly*) Livvy – lives. Livvy – full of life.

She smiles. Clara enters (perhaps she has witnessed this last confession).

Livvy Clara? Where have you been, Clarty-clugs? I've missed you.

Clara is silent.

Livvy Don't be like that, Clara. I want us to be friends.

Clara I've been listening to walls.

Livvy Why don't we bake a cake together? That would be nice.

Clara A funny thing's happened.

Livvy What's that?

Clara The walls have started telling me the future as well. They tell me what's going to happen. They tell me what I should do.

Livvy About what?

Clara just looks at her and then she exits.

Livvy (*calls after her*) No wait, Clara. Please. I want to talk to you. He's gone now. Please. Help me with the cake?

Lights fade.

SCENE SIX

Alex's flat. Mat sits as Alex enters.

Mat Nice smells.

Alex I'm baking a cake. You know you're in your thirties when you have to make your own birthday cake.

Mat Ah, babe. Never mind, I've got a prediction for you.

Alex Oh yes.

Mat You are going to have a great birthday. I can feel some serious cosseting coming your way tonight.

Alex I didn't know you were psychic, Mat.

Mat Oh yeah. It's the family business.

Alex You work in the City.

Mat I'm a futures broker. I deal in the future. My mum's clairsensitive though.

Alex What's that?

Mat She can sense things before they happen. She can't see them, that's clairvoyant, she feels them. In her bones.

Alex That's weird.

Mat It's all bollocks, mind.

Alex You don't believe in it.

Mat Oh. She's in touch with something all right. There's no rest from it. She has manifestations when she's on the bog. It's just she never finds out anything useful. The dead are not a very effective channel of communication.

Alex Why not?

Mat They don't have their finger on the pulse. They never told her that my dad was gonna sling his hook. Which was a bit fucking remiss of them in my opinion.

Alex Perhaps you take after your dad.

Mat Why do you say that?

Alex Hook-slinging. Perhaps you come from a long line of hook-slingers?

Mat We'll have to wait and see, won't we?

Alex Can't you see that far into the future, Mat?

Mat You can never see things for yourself, that would ruin it.

Alex I'd like to know what was going to happen. The gift of hindsight as foresight. I'd like that.

Mat Nah. That's no fun. It's gotta be all up for grabs.

Alex I suppose so.

Mat Well, come on then, Birthday Girl, make your wish.

Alex (*smiles*) I'm only allowed one?

Mat Of course.

Alex Right.

Mat Go on then.

Alex I've made it.

Mat What is it?

Alex I'm not telling.

Mat Oh come on.

Alex No. You just want to know if it involves you.

Mat Course I do.

Alex Well, I'm not telling you.

Mat Which means it does involve me.

Alex When are you going to have your shower?

Mat It involves a very clean me?

Alex You know I only fornicate with shiny, happy people.

Mat Your wish is my command. I won't be long. (*He kisses her.*) You taste vanillery.

Alex Cake mixture.

Mat Can I lick the bowl?

Alex Clean yourself up, Mat.

He exits.

I wish I knew what to wish.

Mat (*off*) What?

Alex Nothing.

SCENE SEVEN

The tapas bar. James and Clootie.

Clootie You're lucky. You believe in people. You help people.

James I'm not lucky. Really I'm not.

Clootie But you care for people.

James No, that's a modern myth. Carers don't actually care. We confine and we contain. We make people sit in the corner and be quiet.

Clootie It's still better than working in a restaurant.

James Most people I know would rather be in a restaurant than a nursing home.

Clootie I don't want to spend my life serving other people dinner. I've got enough problems.

James Like what?

Clootie You don't want to hear all my woes.

James Why not? I'm a professional. I won't be shocked.

Clootie Oh. I don't know. Other people seem to flow through life while I get caught up in the eddies. Like Alex. She was definitely cut on the bias.

James Change. People can do that. That's what I believe in. People's ability to transform themselves.

Clootie (*quietly*) Maybe.

James Are you okay?

Clootie No, not really, James. I can't remember the last time I was okay.

James Oh.

Clootie You see, nine months ago I was going to get married and then my fiancé was arrested for cottaging, oh, you can laugh, it is funny, I know. Now he's come out as a fully fledged homosexual. He holds musical soirées for thin middle-aged men in black leather with handlebar moustaches. Apparently all my friends could see it coming from a mile off but I lived with him for six years and I didn't have one fucking iota of an idea . . . I'm sorry, I didn't want to even mention this tonight. In fact I practised not mentioning this in the mirror before I came out. Sorry.

James Sometimes we hold on to pain for a reason.

Clootie What reason would that be, James?

James You tell me. (*Pause.*) Look at this.

Clootie What is it?

James It's a bone.

Clootie Oh. Yes.

James From my best friend's foot.

Clootie Do you think he might be missing it?

James He's dead.

Clootie Sorry. Shit. I didn't mean to be flippant.

James He killed himself. He went to Hampstead Heath. He doused himself in petrol and then set himself on fire. This is all that was left of him. I carry it with me.

Clootie Oh my God. Hampstead Heath. Why?

James (*impatiently*) I don't know. He lived near there.

Clootie No, sorry. I didn't mean, 'Why Hampstead Heath?' I mean, I suppose Hampstead Heath is as good a place as any. Big open space, etc. No I meant, 'Why did he – ?'

James I don't know. Despair's the usual reason, isn't it? . . . Daniel. We went travelling together all through South America. He was twenty-four when he died.

    Pause.

Clootie Why take it around with you? Like a fetish.

James To remind myself.

Clootie Of him?

James No. Of the alternatives. You always have to be aware of the alternatives.

Clootie I feel a bit sick.

James I think it's a good way to go. In flame.

Clootie I'm a Catholic. We don't hold with burning.

James Do you know what the Parsees do? They bury their dead in the sky. They put the bodies on top of a tower and let the vultures pick them clean. I like that. It's – honest.

Clootie Do you think working with old people has made you a little bit morbid, James?

James Maybe. Do you think serving people dinner has made you a little bit bitter?

Pause.

Clootie All I want is to be more than who I am right now.

James You're too hard on yourself.

Clootie I really like you, James.

James Thank you.

Clootie I want to breathe again. I want to live in the present and breathe more than enough air.

James You will.

Clootie Will I?

James Of course. You're a good person. You deserve a whole lot of air.

Clootie Will you kiss me? Will you kiss me then?

James What?

Clootie I really like you. I'm out of practice but I know I really like you.

James Clootie –

Clootie I just want to – be with someone for a minute. I'm so tired of myself.

James Clootie, I –

Clootie Just for a minute? It doesn't have to last. I'm not looking for lasting commitment.

James Please don't –

Clootie I'm not that repugnant, am I?

James No, of course not.

Clootie Don't tell me you're gay. Now that would be the last screaming irony.

76

James No, I'm not.

Clootie I have put on a bit of weight lately.

James I'm in love with Alex. I love Alex.

Clootie Oh. Yes.

James I'm really sorry. I thought it was obvious.

Clootie (*quickly*) Yes. Yes it was. Sorry. I'm so stupid. I knew it. Exposing this much cleavage always goes to my head.

James When I'm with her, I live in the present. I just don't know how to tell her, Clootie.

Clootie Yes. Yes. Of course.

James She robs me of my voice, my breath. She has such a glow about her. I'm sorry. That all sounds wanky.

Clootie No, no. You've certainly blossomed into metaphor.

James But do you know what I mean?

Clootie Yes. Yes. She shimmers.

James It's such a relief to say these things out loud. I do really like you, Clootie.

Clootie Yes.

James I need to tell her. I'm crawling up the walls with not telling her.

Clootie Then you must. What's the use of having a secret unless you share it?

James I could do.

Pause.

Clootie She's at home now.

James Really?

Clootie Yes.

James Do you think I should?

Clootie What's the alternative? You have to think of the alternative, James.

James You're right.

SCENE EIGHT

Livvy enters. She is mixing a cake. She wipes her brow with her apron. At the same time Alex enters in a different part of the stage with her cake. She makes the same gesture with her hand to her brow. Livvy continues to mix as Alex sets the cake down and puts candles in the cake. Their gestures should almost echo one another.

Livvy It's so hot.

Pause.

This is your first story, child.

They both hear a noise at the same time.

Alex Mat?

Livvy Frank?

The doorbell goes in Alex's flat. At the same time Livvy is gripped with stomach pains. Alex puts down her cake as Livvy drops the bowl she is mixing.

Clarty! Clarty! Please help me. Clarty, get Gramma. Please, Clarty. (*She staggers about and then falls gasping to the ground.*)

Alex's flat.
  James followed by Clootie enters.

James Alex. Hi. You look lovely.

Alex James. Clootie. I didn't expect you back so soon.

Clootie No, change of plan, Alex. Happy birthday. I'm afraid I couldn't get him gift-wrapped at such short notice.

James It's your birthday?

Alex What? Yes.

James Happy birthday. If I'd have known –

Alex No, don't worry. Well, I'll get out of your way.

Clootie No, no, Alex. James wants to look inside your head. Just for fun, for a laugh. Ha, ha, ha, ha.

James (*flustered*) Clootie, – I just wanted a brief word, it won't take long, Alex.

Clootie
  Where do you go to my lovely
  When you're alone in your bed
  Tell me the thoughts that surround you
  I want to look inside your –

God, this song is seminal, isn't it? You know, I think I'm in love with Peter Sarstedt. I love the fact he had only one hit and sank without a trace. I identify with that.

Alex Are you drunk, Clootie?

James I think she is.

Clootie Oh, listen to him, Al. He's such a boring old nurse. He's been totting up how many units of alcohol I've had all evening.

Alex Have you had a good time? Was the tapas nice?

James Yes it was fine.

Clootie Fine! Jamie, that tapas was out of this world. It was definitive tapas, Al, tapas with knobs on, and me and Jamie here got on like a towering bloody inferno.

Alex Clootie, are you all right?

Clootie I'm fine.

James She's fine.

Clootie I'm seething but I'm fine. Do you know that feeling, Al? I don't expect you do. What about you, Jamie? Come seethe with me and be my love and we will all the whatsits prove.

Alex Shall I make some coffee?

Clootie No, coffee's for pouffs, Al.

James Can I just have a quiet word with you, Alex. In private?

Mat enters wearing a towel.

Mat We having a party?

Clootie Yes, we bloody well are. You must be Mat. I've heard all about you and I have to say on first viewing I'm not disappointed, Mat. I'm especially loving your towel arrangement.

Alex This is Clootie. The girl who's sharing with me at the moment.

Mat Nice to meet you, Clootie. Want a drink?

Clootie Oh yes, I do, Mat. A beer please. He's marvellous, isn't he, Al? I can see what you mean. He's like a gladiator.

Alex Yes, well. I think you'd better rein yourself in, Clootie.

Clootie Oh Mat, sorry, this is James. Step forward, James. Don't be shy. Me and James have just had a date, Mat.

Mat All right, mate? Did it go well?

Clootie Fabulous, Mat.

Mat Do you want a beer?

James I've got to get back to work, actually.

Clootie Oh no, James, you must accomplish your mission first. James here has something rather precious to impart to the group.

James No, Clootie. It's okay.

Alex Clootie.

Clootie Oh no, I've got to tell Mat. This is great, Mat – you'll love this. You see, James here wined and dined me tonight. Tapas, no less. Got my juices going, I can tell you. Then he told me he was in love with Alex.

Mat What?

Clootie It's classic, isn't it? Boy, we laughed. I nearly had a hernia.

James I'm sorry, Alex.

Alex All right, that's enough now, Clootie.

James I wanted to tell you. But not like this. I didn't realise you were –

Mat Who is he exactly?

Alex James is a nurse. He looks after my mother.

Clootie They've seen each other every day for the past eight months, Mat.

Mat He's a nurse?

Alex This isn't my fault, Clootie.

Clootie (*turns on Alex for the first time*) You knew how he felt. It was obvious.

James Alex, I want you to forget about all this. It really doesn't matter. It was a mistake. A misunderstanding.

Mat Let me get this right. He's a nurse?

Alex No, wait a minute, James.

Clootie Geriatric, yes.

Mat Have you slept with him, Alex?

Alex Don't get all territorial with me, Mat. Save that for your wife.

Mat I've always been straight with you, Alex.

Clootie What did you think, Alex, you'd get rid of two lame ducks in one go?

James I'm not a lame duck, Clootie.

Mat No, you're a fucking nurse.

Clootie I told you how much I liked him. This was a big deal for me, Alex.

Mat He shovels old ladies' shit for a living, love, I think you're better off without him.

James What would you know about it?

Mat Hark at Florence Nightingale. Keep your hair on, Florence.

James Alex. I can't get you out of my head. I think about you all the time.

Mat You're not her type, Florence. Too lame. And there's definitely something of the duck about you.

Alex Shut up, Mat.

James Yes, shut up.

Mat Ooh. Quack, quack.

James Alex, I think I should leave.

Alex No, James, we should sort this out.

Clootie You're in your element now, aren't you, Alex? With men falling for you left, right and centre.

Alex Don't blame me because you've fucked up your life. Because your fiancé ran off with another man.

Mat He what?

Alex I'm sick of you, Clootie. I'm sick of picking you up when you're down.

Clootie You don't pick me up. You trample all over me.

Alex You shouldn't assume people are happy just because they don't moan as much as you.

Clootie Next to you I'm invisible.

Mat You're pretty audible though.

Alex I'm thirty-six. I have no children. My lover is married.

James You're thirty-six?

Alex What?

James I mean, you really don't look it.

Alex Oh yes, I feel great, James, I'm at the pinnacle. I've peaked. I'm thirty-six and my mother is dying.

Clootie You don't like your mother. You never have done.

Alex That's not true.

Clootie Well, look after her then.

Alex I can't. She needs full-time care. Doesn't she, James? Doesn't she?

Clootie Don't ask him, he's a fucking nutter. He's got this bone he carries around. He's probably got jars of pickled baby at home. And he's got scars all up his arms. I didn't like to ask, well, you don't, do you?

James You bitch.

Clootie You're welcome to him, Alex.

James Did you set me up with her, Alex?

Alex I didn't do anything.

James I thought I made it obvious, how I felt.

Clootie Of course you knew, Alex. I bet he dribbled all over you.

Mat She plays things close to her chest though, don't you, Alex?

Alex All right. All right. So what if I knew. He likes me. They all like me, isn't that right, Clootie? I'm very desirable. Right up there in the pecking order. But open me up and I'm full of shit. Is this what you want to hear, what you all want to hear?

James I love you, Alex.

Mat You're on a losing wicket, mate.

Alex Oh yes, Mat, and you're speaking from such a position of strength. We're not having a good time, Mat. Let's face it, we're just not.

    Pause.

Mat (*coolly*) No. You're right. I think we'd better call it a day.

Alex What?

Clootie I thought he was going to leave his wife, Alex.

Mat You don't want me, Alex. I'm just a bit of rough to you. Who earns a fuck of a lot of money.

Alex No, I –

Mat There was a moment back there when I could have wavered for you. But I don't like being underestimated either, you see.

Clootie You tell her, Mat.

Mat Besides I'm beginning to feel a tad underdressed.

Alex I want you to leave Katherine.

Mat I can't do that.

Clootie You mess people up, Alex. It's a great talent of yours.

Alex Do you love me?

Mat Katherine's pregnant.

Alex What?

James Jesus.

Mat Which makes everything different. I'm sorry. But we both knew –

Alex And when were you planning to tell me that?

Mat I was waiting to find the right moment.

Clootie Oh dear. I don't think you've found it yet.

Mat Why don't you shut up, you fat cunt?

Clootie I'm not fat.

Mat I'm going.

Clootie Oh stay, Mat. Aren't you going to fuck her till she's senseless? For old time's sake.

Mat lashes out and hits Clootie. She is knocked to the ground.

Mat I'm sorry. I don't know you, but you had that coming to you from such a long way off.

Pause.
James goes to help her up.

Clootie I'm fine.

Mat I'm sorry, Alex. (*He kisses her lightly on the forehead*) Mind how you go on the roads, eh? (*He exits.*)

Alex I can't breathe in here.

Clootie I'm crap at parties. I always end up on the floor.

Alex Get out, please.

Clootie Don't worry, I'm going. (*She exits.*)

James You knew I felt this way, didn't you?

Alex Yes.

James You deserve better than him.

Alex No, James, I don't deserve anything.

James I want to be with you.

Alex James –

James I think we could –

Alex I would never find someone like you attractive. I'm sorry.

James Right. Yes.

Alex I'm sorry. James?

James What?

Alex Was I wrong to put my mother into care?

James I can't answer that.

Alex Please.

James You entrusted your mother to my care, Alex. And I could do anything to her. There are hours and hours when I could do anything to her. I don't, but things go through my head. When you look after the dispossessed, they drag you down, you see.

   Pause.

Anyway. I've got to get back – see to – yes.

   He exits.
    Alex is left. She stands a minute and looks at the cake. She starts to light the candles.

SCENE TEN

In another part of the stage Alex's mother shuffles on. She stops. Suddenly she notices that she is wearing tap shoes. She tries out a few steps as Alex lights the candles. She looks up at the audience, smiles a huge smile. She is transformed; there is no sign of her stroke. She launches into a tap routine. Music: 'I Could Have Danced All Night'. She is all smiles. Alex finishes lighting her candles. Alex gets up and walks out. The tap routine finishes. Lights fade.

Lights up on Livvy as before; she is collapsed on the ground. Clara is standing over her.

Livvy Clara. Please help me. Please get Gramma for me. I'm burning up, Clara.

Pause.

Please. My baby. I'm losing my baby.

Clara I hate you, Livvy.

Livvy No, Clara.

Clara And the walls told me what to do.

Livvy Clara –

Clara I'm going to haunt you till you die.

Livvy No please, Clara. GRAMMA! GRAMMA! HELP! HELP ME PLEASE!

Clara begins to stamp. She drowns out Livvy's cries. Her stamping becomes ryhthmic, like a dance. Livvy collapses completely on the floor. At the same time, Alex comes back on. She has a large packet of paracetomol. She kneels on the floor at the same time as Livvy and calmly pushes the pills out of their blister packets. She counts them out.

Livvy Suddenly I am rising above myself.

Gramma What's happened, Clara?

Livvy I can see myself – (*She looks at Alex.*) – so small and lost down there.

Clara The stones are crying out to me, Gramma. Make the stones stop.

Livvy And Gramma and Clara around me –

Gramma We're losing her, Clara.

Livvy – as if from a great height.

Gramma Do something, Clara. We must do something.

Clara I'm sorry, Gramma. I didn't mean to. I didn't mean it. The walls told me to.

Livvy I want the child to live so much.

Gramma I don't know what to do, Clara.

Clara Make her have an Epiphany, Gramma. Make her blessed.

Livvy I'm shooting up and up.

Gramma My poor lost girl, come back to me.

Clara Make her come back, Gramma.

Livvy The land cannot hold me.

Clara We must breathe on her. Breathe her back to life. Do it, Gramma. Breathe her full of fire.

Gramma It's no good, Clara.

Clara I'm sorry, Livvy. I didn't mean it, Livvy.

Alex picks up a handful of pills.

Livvy I am being swallowed by the sky.

Clara I love you, Livvy.

Gramma Pray, Clara. We must pray for her.

Clara Holy Ghost come down on my sister. Please.

Livvy I'm leaving myself behind. (*Livvy walks past Alex towards the birthday cake.*)

Clara Please! I didn't mean her to die. Livvy live Livvy live Livvy live Livvy live Livvy live Livvy live Livvy live –

Livvy blows out the candles. She watches the next.

No. (*a small whine*)

Alex sits up abruptly. Anne speaks as if to a child. .

Alex Mother?

Mother I'm here, Alex.

Alex I want my mother. (*She starts to cry. Throughout the next she doesn't respond directly to Anne.*)

Mother Shsh. Shsh. It'll be all right. Everything will be all right.

Alex I'm sorry. I'm sorry. I'm sorry.

Mother It's all right. None of it matters. Not a bit of it matters.

Alex I'm sorry.

Mother I know you are.

Alex I don't know what to do.

Mother We'll get that fringe cut for a start. That'll make you feel better.

Alex I'm lost. Please help me.

Mother Put them all back in the box. That's it. I won't stand for it. What would your father say.

Alex I'm sorry. (*She picks up the pills and puts them back in the box.*)

Mother That's it. That's better. Go and wash your face. Don't listen to any of them. They can all go to hell. There. Now. It'll all feel better in the morning.

Alex Yes.

Mother Off you go then.

Alex I'm sorry.

Mother Off you go. There's a good girl.

Alex gets up slowly and walks off.

Livvy Come on then, Annie. Are you ready?

Mother/Gramma Ready as I'll ever be.

Clara No wait, Gramma. You mustn't go too. You haven't heard my secret yet.

Mother/Gramma No time for secrets now, Clara. I'm exhausted. Let's have a bit of hush.

Livvy Here sit here, Annie.

Mother/Gramma It's all the dancing you see. It's worn me out. (*She lies down.*) That's better. Take the weight off my poor old feet.

Livvy That's it, you rest now.

Mother/ Gramma shuts her eyes as if to sleep. Livvy exits.

Clara No, you can't leave me. You can't both leave me. Gramma.

She shakes her. Gramma doesn't respond.

Gramma. Listen to me, Gramma. Please. I've got a baby too. I've got Livvy's baby inside of me now. And my baby will live. My baby will live for Livvy. (*Clara exits.*)

SCENE TWELVE

The nursing home.
Anne is lying in her bed as James enters

James Well, I asked her nicely, Annie. And she wasn't having any of it. I'm just not glossy enough, Annie. I'm a bloody fool. So I wondered if maybe I could fuck you instead. In for a penny, in for a pound, eh? It's just you and me, kid. Come on, get up, old lady. Let's be having you.

He realises something is wrong. Feels for her pulse. Anne is dead.

Shit. Shit. Shit.

Pause.

The things women do to avoid sleeping with me. Don't you worry yourself, Annie. You're fine now. Just fine. You've renewed youself, Annie. All your molecules have re-arranged themselves. You've changed gear, haven't you? Now you'll be brand new again.

Pause.

I wonder if I might have the pleasure of this dance? We can dance the night away. You'd like that, wouldn't you? Right little rocker. We just need the finishing touches. (*He exits and gets two sparklers out and lights them.*) I bought these for you. But I was just waiting for the right moment. Annie you are absolutely the person I want to be with now. You are my dream date for this evening. There. Look at them sparkle, Annie. Do you want to hold them? No, you need both your hands for dancing. I know.

You look magnificent, Annie. Let's dance. (*He lifts her limp body.*) We're spinning, Annie. We're spinning with the sparklers.

He exits with her.

SCENE THIRTEEN

Alex's flat. Some time later.
  Alex collects the framed photograph of Livvy Unwin.
She places it. Clootie enters.

Clootie I didn't expect you to be here. I just came to get my things together.

Alex Tie up all the loose ends. Go ahead.

Clootie I'm sorry about your mother.

Alex I have no idea what to say when people say that to me.

Clootie That's okay.

Alex I didn't love my mother, Clootie, but she was still my mother.

Clootie Yes.

Alex I nearly lost it completely, you know, that night.

Clootie I'm sorry for the things I said.

Alex You shouldn't be sorry if you meant them.

Clootie I was drunk.

Alex But you know what you said.

Clootie Yes.

Alex I hate you for that night, Clootie. But you were right, what you said, some of the things you said, you were right.

  Pause.

You look better.

Clootie I feel better. Sorry.

Alex Why should you be sorry?

Clootie shrugs.

Can you keep a secret?

Clootie No, I'm terrible at secrets, you know that.

Alex I'm pregnant.

Clootie Oh my God.

Alex Mat's parting shot. I'm not going to tell him. Anyway I haven't decided what to do about it yet.

Clootie Oh.

Alex I've offended your Catholic sensibilities.

Clootie No. No. Anyway I'm giving up being a Catholic. I'm going to get hypnotherapy for it . . . You must do what you think best.

Alex I want to feel like I – deserve it . . . I've taken my mum's house off the market. I want to spend some time – I've been going through all her things, you were right. Livvy Unwin was my great-great-aunt.

Clootie What?

Alex The girl in the photograph, she died in 1908, the year the photograph was taken. Ectopic pregnancy.

Clootie How did you find out?

Alex There were letters and stuff. Family papers. My great-grandmother was mad apparently. Clara.

Clootie Well that's what happens to women, isn't it? They go mad or they die in childbirth.

Alex Looks like I'm heading for the double whammy.

Clootie You'll be all right, my lovely. I'd better get started.

Clootie exits. After a moment Livvy appears. Alex looks at her picture as Livvy speaks to her. At the same time Clootie re-enters as Clara and sits as in the first scene.

Livvy You are not lost.

Alex Clootie?

Livvy You will always know who your mother is.

Alex touches her stomach.

I've been saving up my words for you.

Alex takes the picture and sits next to the wall. She curls up to it as if she were listening to it.

This is your first story.

SCENE FOURTEEN

Frank walks past Livvy and Alex towards Clara.

Clara You came back!

Frank I remembered it.

Clara What?

Frank The special thing I do.

Clara I thought you might.

Frank Lie down, Clara.

Clara Oh yes. That's right.

Frank It's a pretty name, Clara. So pretty. (*He starts to fuck her quite gently.*) Am I hurting you?

Clara No.

Frank I don't want to hurt you.

Clara No. I like it.

He gains momentum.

You're breathing all over me. Yes. Breathing like fire.
I've been waiting for something like this for so long. Yes.
I like it. You make me feel wise.

He comes. Gets up.

Frank I've got to be going.

Clara Oh. All right.

Frank Goodbye, Clara.

Clara Goodbye.

He exits. (She sits there. She stares ahead.) Won't tell
anyone about this. Nobody at all. (*She looks at the
walls.*) Shsh. Shsh. Shsh.

Lights fade.